PowerPhonics™

# What a Whale!

## Learning the WH Sound

Ilse Battistoni

The Rosen Publishing Group's
PowerKids Press™
New York

# What is a whale?

A whale is an animal.

Where does a whale live?

A whale lives in the ocean.

What color is a whale?

A whale can be gray.

A whale can be white.

A whale can be black and white.

Why does a whale have a tail?

A whale has a tail to help it swim.

# Word List

whale

what

where

white

why

# Instructional Guide

**Note to Instructors:**
One of the essential skills that enable a young child to read is the ability to associate letter-sound symbols and blend these sounds to form words. Phonics instruction can teach children a system that will help them decode unfamiliar words and, in turn, enhance their word-recognition skills. We offer a phonics-based series of books that are easy to read and understand. Each book pairs words and pictures that reinforce specific phonetic sounds in a logical sequence. Topics are based on curriculum goals appropriate for early readers in the areas of science, social studies, and health.

**Letter/Sound: wh** – Write and pronounce the phrase *white whale*. Have the child underline the initial **wh** in each word. Have them give **wh** words that rhyme with the following: *smile, sale, kite, heat, eel, ten, sky.*
• Pronounce pairs of words and have the child name the word in each pair that begins with **wh**: *where – she, child – why, this – what, whale – sheep,* etc.

**Phonics Activities:** Tell a story, pausing at intervals to hold up a consonant card. Have the child supply an appropriate word that begins with the consonant displayed. (Example: *Willie the whale liked to play in the* **s** _____ [sea].)
• Have the child name words that have the same long vowel sound in oral sentences such as the following: *Jim can make a picture of a whale. Come and take a piece of cake. It's time to rest for a while. We can hike up a high hill. Some kids came to watch the game. Pete will feed his kitten.* As the child responds, list the words with long vowel sounds. List all the **wh** words and identify their vowel sounds.
• Pronounce the following **wh** words: *who, whose, whole.* Ask the child to name the sound they hear at the beginning of each word. List the three words on a chalkboard or dry-erase board. Have the child name the two letters they see at the beginning of each word. Lead them to generalize that **wh** followed by **vowel o** often has the same sound as **h**.

Additional Resources:
• Crewe, Sabrina. *The Whale*. Orlando, FL: Raintree Steck-Vaughn Publishers, 1997.
• Davies, Nicola. *Big Blue Whale*. Cambridge, MA: Candlewick Press, 1997.
• Gibbons, Gail. *Whales*. New York: Holiday House, Inc., 1991.
• Tracqui, Valerie. *The Whale: Giant of the Ocean*. Watertown, MA: Charlesbridge Publishing, Inc., 1995.

Published in 2002 by The Rosen Publishing Group, Inc.
29 East 21st Street, New York, NY 10010

Copyright © 2002 by The Rosen Publishing Group, Inc.

Book Design: Haley Wilson

Photo Credits: Cover, pp. 7, 11 (bottom), 17 © Gerard Lacz/Animals Animals; p. 3 © James Watt/Animals Animals; pp. 5, 19 © Johnny Johnson/Animals Animals; p. 9 © Stephen Simpson/FPG International; pp. 11 (top left), 13 © Cliff Hollenbeck/International Stock; pp. 11 (top right), 15 © Zig Leszczynski/Animals Animals; p. 21 © David Fleetham/FPG International.

Library of Congress Cataloging-in-Publication Data

Battistoni, Ilse.
    What a whale! : learning the WH sound / Ilse Battistoni.— 1st ed.
      p. cm. — (Power phonics/phonics for the real world)
    ISBN 0-8239-5929-5 (lib. bdg.)
    ISBN 0-8239-8274-2 (pbk.)
    ISBN 0-8239-9242-X
    1. Whales—Juvenile literature.  2. English
    language—Consonants—Juvenile literature. [1. Whales.]    I. Title.
    II. Series.
    QL737.C4 B35 2002
    599.5—dc21
                                              2001000180

Manufactured in the United States of America